ISAAC ASIMOV'S
Library of the Universe

Space Garbage

by Isaac Asimov

Gareth Stevens Children's Books
LONDON • MILWAUKEE

A note from the editors: In the United States and other places — including this book — a billion is the number represented by 1 followed by nine zeros — 1,000,000,000. In other countries, including Britain, this number is often called a 'thousand million', and one billion would then be represented by 1 followed by 12 zeros — 1,000,000,000,000: a million million, which is called a 'trillion' in this book.

The reproduction rights to all photographs and illustrations in this book are controlled by the individuals or institutions credited on page 32 and may not be reproduced without their permission.

British Library Cataloguing in Publication Data

Asimov, Isaac, 1920-
   Space garbage.
   I. Title II. Series
   629.41

   ISBN 0-83687-098-0

A Gareth Stevens Children's Books edition

Edited, designed, and produced by
Gareth Stevens Children's Books   31 Newington Green, London N16 9PU

First published in the United States and Canada in 1989 by Gareth Stevens, Inc.
First published in the United Kingdom in 1990 by Gareth Stevens Children's Books

Cover painting © Pat Rawlings

Project editor: Mark Sachner
Designer: Laurie Shock
Research editor: Scott Enk
Picture research: Matthew Groshek
Editor (UK): Dee Turner

Technical advisers and consulting editors: Julian Baum and Francis Reddy

Printed in the United States of America

1 2 3 4 5 6 7 8 9 96 95 94 93 92 91 90

CONTENTS

Nowadays, we have seen close-up views of all the known planets except for distant Pluto. We have seen dead volcanoes on Mars and live ones on Io, one of Jupiter's moons. We have studied Triton, the moon of far-off Neptune. We have detected strange objects no-one knew anything about till recently: quasars, pulsars, black holes. We have studied stars not only by light, but by other kinds of radiation: infra-red, ultraviolet, x-rays, radio waves. We have even detected tiny particles called neutrinos that are given off by the stars.

We have actually explored our Solar system, especially the part very close to Earth. We have sent many, many rockets into space, most of which continue to orbit Earth even after they stop working. The result is that nearby space is filled with space debris — or 'space garbage', as some people call it. In this book we will take a look at this rubbish in space and consider why it is important.

Isaac Asimov

Earth's Orbiting Junkyard

We have placed many satellites in orbit around Earth since the late 1950s. Most of them are still circling our planet, even if they're no longer working. At least 80 satellites have broken up into fragments. With time, the fragments break up further. There are now more than 40,000 pieces of space debris, each at least the size of a golf ball, circling Earth.

There are billions of tinier pieces, like small specks of paint. Some debris eventually floats down to Earth, but more is being formed than settles down, and the total amount of 'space junk' is steadily increasing.

Satellites and orbital debris swarm around Earth in record numbers. Opposite: This artist's impression is based on a computer image of objects tracked close to our planet.

Below: Thin rings of debris also orbit Earth further out in space, beyond the 'ball' of debris clustered closer to our planet. A NASA computer made this picture.

Traces on Other Worlds — A Monument or a Mess?

Spacecraft have also landed on the Moon, and 12 human beings have walked on its soil. Parts of the spacecraft have been left behind, and other litter has been left at various sites on the Moon. There are also several spacecraft on Mars and on Venus. The USSR recently launched a probe designed to land equipment on the Martian satellite Phobos.

This means we will have placed material on four different worlds. Some of it may be looked on as monuments to Earth's space programmes — the United States flags and plaques on the Moon, for instance. But lots of it is really junk.

Each of the Apollo Moon missions left behind scientific packages, including instruments that watch for 'Moon quakes' and mirrors that reflect laser beams from Earth.

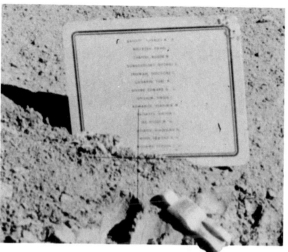

Above: A small memorial to the US astronauts and Soviet cosmonauts who gave their lives in the cause of exploring space, left on the Moon by Apollo 15 astronauts.

Left: A replica of the olive branch — a symbol of peace — taken to the Moon aboard Apollo 11.

Lunar litter —
the last trace of humanity?

Suppose that a nuclear war wiped out humanity. Gradually wind, water, and remaining forms of life would destroy what is left of our cities. If visitors from some other civilization came millions of years later, they would find no sign that humanity ever ruled Earth. But on the Moon there will still be the litter our astronauts left behind between 1969 and 1972, looking almost as it did to begin with. That 'junk' may then be our final monument.

Further Frontiers — Junk in the Cosmos

We will continue exploring space. There seems to be no doubt about that. But it also seems that we human beings can't go anywhere without leaving behind some of the materials we have produced. On Earth, we have filled the land surfaces with rubbish; we have polluted the oceans with all kinds of waste, and we are filling the atmosphere with dust and poisonous gases.

Are we gradually going to pollute space and neighbouring worlds, too? And will we continue to do so as we explore further? Will we leave traces of ourselves wherever we go? And will these traces be in the form of useless and unsightly junk?

Above: Time to take out the trash! Astronauts aboard the US Skylab space station pack up their rubbish.

Below: A barge carrying its cargo of refuse towards the sea. The cars on the bridge give an idea of how big the barge is.

Improperly launched rubbish bags alarmed cosmonauts on Salyut 6 when they seemed to follow the space station.

Some 'space garbage' really _is_ garbage!

In 1978, two cosmonauts in the Soviet Salyut 6 space station dumped two bags of rubbish into space. Later, ground controllers told the cosmonauts to check out two nearby 'unidentified flying objects'. One man looked out of the window — and was shocked to see two dark, round objects keeping pace with the spacecraft! Only after a few hair-raising seconds did he realize that the scary, strange-looking 'UFOs' were merely the rubbish bags they had thrown out.

For several nights following the launch of Skylab in 1973, several 'extra' satellites streaked across the night sky — parts of the rocket that launched the huge space laboratory.

Left: Radar dishes such as these are part of a worldwide electronic 'trash- tracking' network.

From their underground post beneath Cheyenne Mountain in Colorado, members of the US Space Surveillance Center keep track of nearly 7,000 bits of space junk.

Tracking the Trash

Space debris is not just a matter of messiness. It is important to know where it is, especially the big pieces. After all, if we send additional satellites into space, we don't want to put them into an orbit where they will collide with a piece of debris and be put out of action. That is one reason we send radio waves into space — to track the trash.

These radio waves bounce off satellites and debris so that people on Earth know the exact location of each object, whether working or dead, and where it is going. This helps us choose a good orbit for the next satellite.

But, one day soon, we may run out of safe orbits!

Spacewalking — Is It Safe?

Space contains speeding meteoroids, most of them the size of a grain of sand. They move at many kilometres a second, and even a small one can puncture a space suit and kill an astronaut. But space is vast, and so far no 'killer meteoroid' has struck any astronaut.

Space debris is equally dangerous. A fleck of paint struck a space shuttle in 1983 and chipped the windshield, which had to be replaced at a cost of about £30,000. A slightly larger object might have punctured the windshield and killed the entire crew. The more debris we put up there, the greater the danger.

Solar wind — another kind of debris

The Sun is always hurling out its own 'debris'— electrically charged subatomic particles. This is called the solar wind. The radiation is harmful, though not enough to threaten astronauts. But, every once in a while, there is an explosion on the Sun called a solar flare. Then the number of particles rises to a deadly level. There was an enormous flare in 1972 between the two Moon missions. Luckily, there were no astronauts in space at the time.

Top: Many tiny craters like this were found on the Solar Maximum satellite after its return to Earth in 1984. High-speed flakes of paint did all the damage!

Bottom: Atomic particles streaming from the Sun leave their marks in Moon rocks, like these. Earth's atmosphere protects us from these particles.

Opposite: The US space shuttle Challenger. A tiny fleck of paint made this microscopic crater in the craft's window — a potentially dangerous cosmic encounter.

Satellites — Debris We Depend On

We could stop leaving debris if we stopped sending up satellites, but we really can't do that. Since we began sending them up in the 1950s, we have come to depend on satellites. For instance, some satellites help us predict the weather, tell us about Earth's cloud cover, and track storms such as hurricanes.

Some satellites make it possible for us to send messages across oceans. Some allow ships to know exactly where they are at all times. Some make it possible for us to study Earth, its soil, its oceans, its crops.

We must have satellites, and so we'll continue to end up with their debris.

Above: This orbiting 'crystal ball', LAGEOS, may one day help us predict earthquakes. Scientists bounce laser beams off its hundreds of reflectors to measure movements in Earth's crust.

Right: The European Infra-red Space Observatory (ISO) will measure the heat of newborn stars.

Satellites are our 'eyes in the sky', providing us with a way to see the weather all around our planet. Weather-watching satellites (left) have saved many lives by letting us see how dangerous storms, such as Hurricane Juan (below), develop and move.

What If . . . ? — Skylab and Other Near Misses

Space debris can even be dangerous to us here on Earth. As debris passes through thin wisps of upper air, it gradually comes close to Earth and finally enters the main atmosphere. Small pieces just burn up. But large pieces can reach Earth's surface. Nearly three-quarters of them will splash into the ocean, but some may hit land. Parts of a Soviet satellite, Cosmos 954, fell on northern Canada in 1978.

Also in 1978, increased activity on the surface of the Sun heated up Earth's atmosphere, causing it to expand. This increased the atmosphere's 'drag' on the US Skylab satellite, until parts of Skylab finally came down on July 11, 1979, hitting western Australia. It's not very likely that pieces of satellites will hit buildings or people. But someday a lump of debris may do so.

A plume of gas rises above the Sun's surface. This kind of activity can expand Earth's atmosphere — and bring down satellites in low orbits.

Opposite, top left: Cosmos 954, a Soviet satellite that fell on Canada in 1978, scattered radioactive debris that had to be found and removed.

Opposite, top right: Part of a water tank recovered when Skylab broke apart in Earth's atmosphere.

Only about 30% of Earth's surface is land, and only about 1% of this land has large concentrations of people. So, if a large piece of debris falls to Earth, the chances are about 1 in 333 that it might do serious harm to human beings. This means that if a large piece of space debris falls to Earth only once every 10 years, then the odds are that it will be some 3,000 years or more before a piece causes serious harm to people on Earth.

Of course, by bad luck, a piece might hit next year. As our planet's population goes up and cities spread outward, the chances of damage or harm increase. On the other hand, if we clean up space, the chances will decrease. It's that simple.

Opposite: The Skylab Orbiting Workshop, launched by the US in 1973.

Left: Satellites that fall to Earth burn and break apart in our atmosphere. Natural space debris also leaves glowing trails as it streaks to Earth as meteors.

Above: The bright plume of a solar flare leaps above the Sun's surface.

Solar flares — life-and-death questions remain

The explosions on the Sun that expel a deadly tide of charged particles take place at odd times. Scientists don't always know what causes these solar flares or when they'll take place. This means that astronauts working on a space station, for instance, will never know when to expect these dangerous events — so the station will have to be shielded at all times. After further study, flares may become predictable, and life in space will become safer.

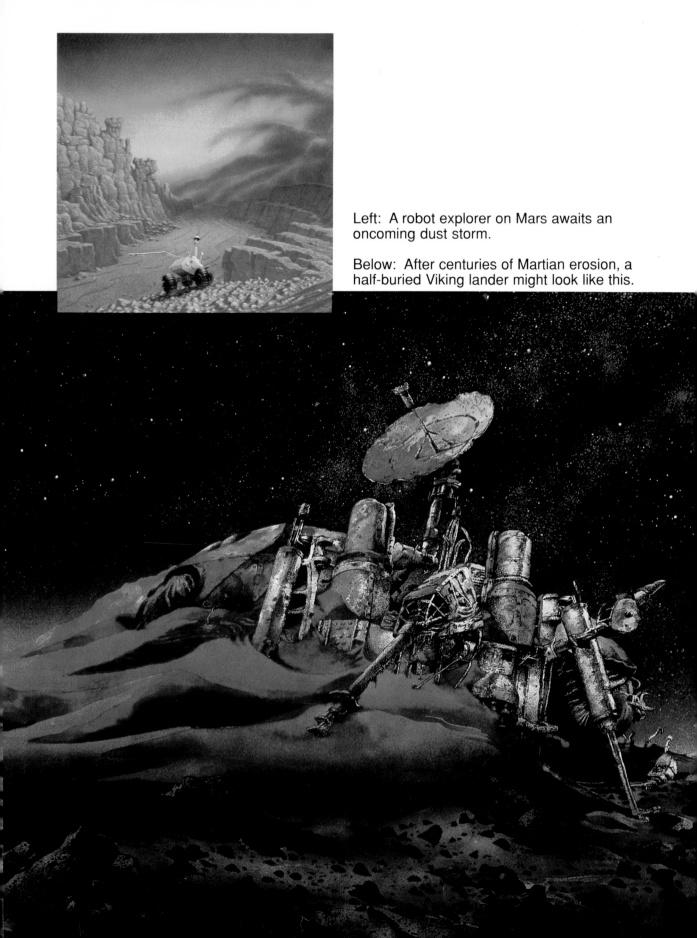

Left: A robot explorer on Mars awaits an oncoming dust storm.

Below: After centuries of Martian erosion, a half-buried Viking lander might look like this.

Cosmic Litter — Will It Last Forever?

Much of the debris in nearby space will return harmlessly to Earth. In this way, nearby space is 'self-cleaning'. Further from Earth, space also cleans up after us. The probes that have landed on Venus will be exposed to very high temperatures and the action of strong winds, and they will eventually be reduced to dust. On Mars, sandstorms might do the same, but more slowly.

But, on places like our Moon and Phobos, there is no atmosphere to wear down our litter. On these worlds, any junk left behind could last for millions of years. So it is important to remember that, under some conditions, our junk may be around forever.

Of course, if we set up a permanent lunar base, we can at least keep the Moon clean. But what about the other litter we leave in the cosmos?

A Soviet Venera probe rests on the surface of Venus. The probe stopped transmitting an hour after landing, its electronics destroyed by the planet's tremendous heat.

Cosmic rays — the debris of a dying star?

Cosmic ray particles are more penetrating and deadly than solar wind particles. Usually there are not enough to be dangerous. Astronomers think many originate with supernovas, or violently exploding stars. A nearby supernova may make space deadly for a while. Stars do not often explode as supernovas, and only a few stars are close enough to be dangerous. But a supernova explosion is unpredictable, so we don't know just when danger might come.

?

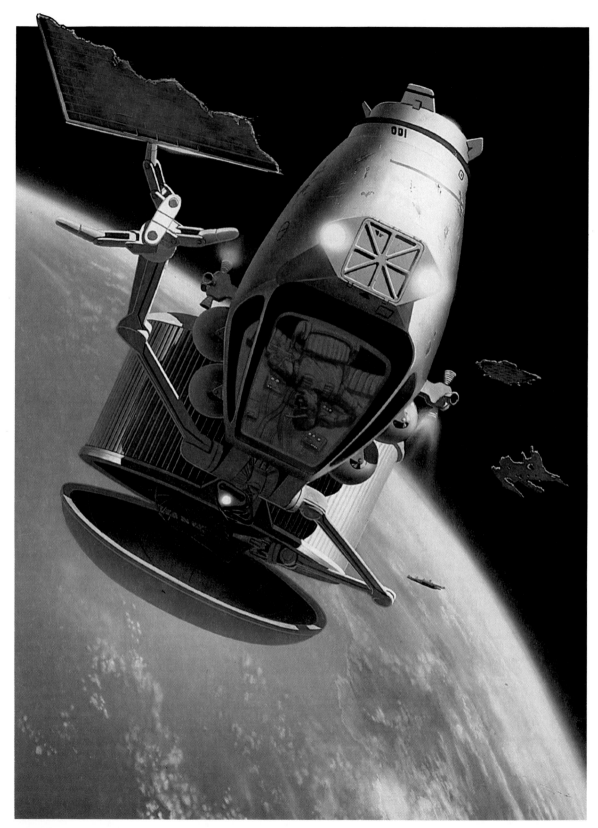

Low orbits are the most littered with space junk. Perhaps one day orbiting 'refuse collectors' will be used to clean up these rubbish-filled orbits.

Learning to Keep Space Clean

If we let too much debris accumulate around our planet, it might be impossible for us to find safe orbits for future satellites. One of the tasks of some space shuttle missions is to pick up satellites that aren't working and repair them or remove them.

We will have to learn now to send up satellites that don't easily fall apart into fragments and that survive collisions with fragments already in space. Perhaps we will work out a way to sweep up the larger pieces.

So far, nothing much has been done. If we continue to do nothing, increasing debris may put an end to space exploration once and for all.

A black hole — the ultimate rubbish dump? Advanced space civilizations may use 'small' black holes to dispose of their junk.

Beyond the Solar System

In 1957 the USSR sent up Sputnik 1, Earth's first artificial satellite. That wasn't so long ago. But today we have sent space probes out beyond the planets. The Pioneer 10 probe is now moving far beyond the known Solar system and is still sending back messages. It could do so until after the year 2000, but eventually its energy will run out and it will stop working. It will continue moving outward, however, as a far-flung piece of junk.

Other probes will follow, and one day there might be large numbers of such dead objects sailing through interstellar space for countless millions of years. Of what value will these objects be during their endless journey into the cosmos?

Opposite: Earth's deep-space probes sail beyond the outer reaches of our Solar system. This artist's impression shows Voyager 2 (foreground), with Pioneers 10 and 11 off to the right. Also shown (background) is the path of Voyager 1, which passed through the plane of Saturn's rings at a steep angle and headed 'up' and away from the Solar system.

Skimming the stars

Where are the deep-space probes going? One of them, Voyager 2, continues to move outward after taking pictures of Uranus in 1986 and of Neptune in 1989. In about 40,000 years, it will skim past a red dwarf star named Ross 248 and be only 1.65 light-years from it. That's still almost 16 trillion km — not very close! But it's the closest Voyager 2 will come to any star other than our Sun in the first million years of its journey.

Above: The time is 100 million years from now. The place is somewhere in interstellar space. Voyager 2, now a derelict craft cratered by the impact of countless tiny meteoroids, drifts in the vicinity of a red supergiant star.

Right: This plaque aboard Pioneer 10 includes images of a woman and a man (the man's hand raised in a sign of good will). A diagram of the Solar system shows Pioneer leaving Earth, flying by Mars and Jupiter, and sailing into interstellar space.

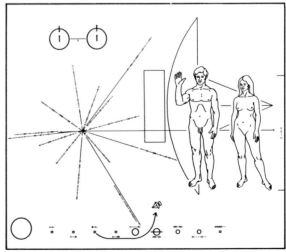

And Finally . . .

Some deep-space probes carry with them plaques giving information about Earth and its location. Some carry records with various sounds on them, including the sounds of humans speaking. The idea behind this is that someday — perhaps millions of years from now — intelligent beings from other worlds may come across such distant debris and discover the plaques and records.

Will it be dangerous to attract their attention? Probably not; there's no reason to think that intelligent beings from distant planets will be unfriendly.

Perhaps even future human beings living in settlements in distant space may discover the plaques and records. Will they be able to understand the information sent out so many millions of years ago? Or will they be so distant from Earth in time and space that they will wonder how beings so much like them could have lived on such a 'strange' planet like Earth?

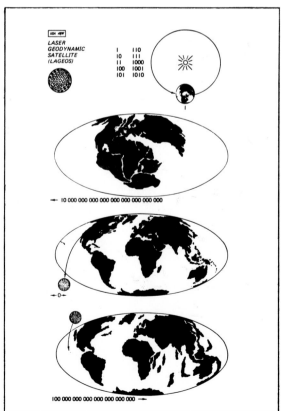

Right: A plaque aboard LAGEOS (see page 14) shows three views of Earth's shifting continents: one of the distant past; one of the present; and one of the distant future.

Fact File: Not All 'Space Rubbish' Is Rubbish!

Like many other things, much of what we send into space — or what comes our way from space — can be good or bad. Satellites can help warn us about dangerous storms. But they can be dangerous themselves when pieces of them fall to Earth. In the same way, meteorites might cause damage on Earth if they fall in the wrong place, but meteorites can also help us learn more about the Universe. Here are some benefits and dangers of different kinds of 'space rubbish'.

A meteoroid hits Earth's atmosphere.

Solar-propelled sailing.

Mining the asteroids.

Kind of 'Space Rubbish'
Meteoroids, meteorites and asteroids
Piloted spacecraft
Satellites
Solar wind and solar flares
Strategic Defence Initiative ('Star Wars') anti-nuclear satellite system
Unpiloted space probes (Hubble Space Telescope, Pioneer, Mariner, Voyager, etc.)

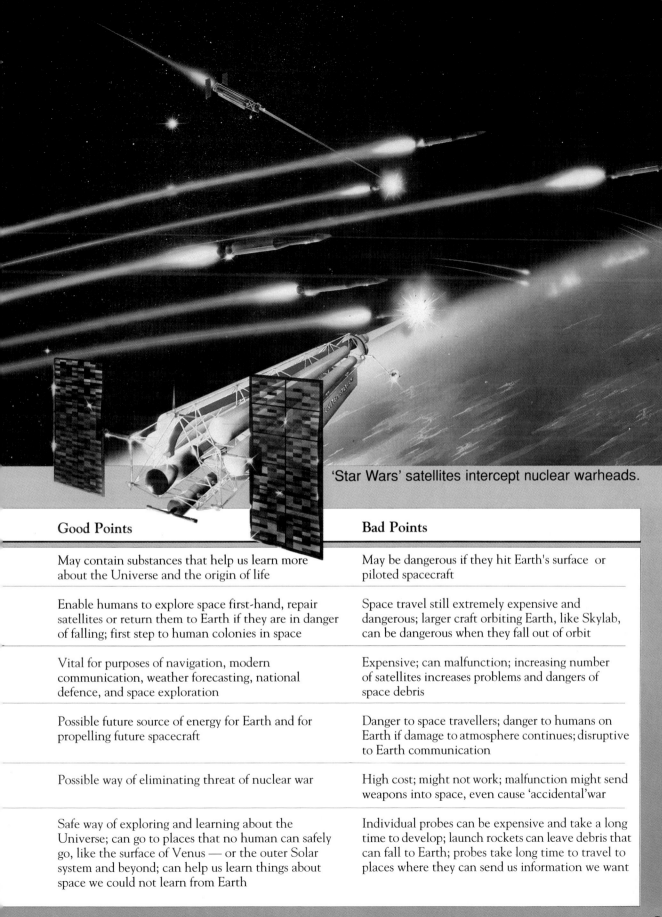

'Star Wars' satellites intercept nuclear warheads.

Good Points	Bad Points
May contain substances that help us learn more about the Universe and the origin of life	May be dangerous if they hit Earth's surface or piloted spacecraft
Enable humans to explore space first-hand, repair satellites or return them to Earth if they are in danger of falling; first step to human colonies in space	Space travel still extremely expensive and dangerous; larger craft orbiting Earth, like Skylab, can be dangerous when they fall out of orbit
Vital for purposes of navigation, modern communication, weather forecasting, national defence, and space exploration	Expensive; can malfunction; increasing number of satellites increases problems and dangers of space debris
Possible future source of energy for Earth and for propelling future spacecraft	Danger to space travellers; danger to humans on Earth if damage to atmosphere continues; disruptive to Earth communication
Possible way of eliminating threat of nuclear war	High cost; might not work; malfunction might send weapons into space, even cause 'accidental' war
Safe way of exploring and learning about the Universe; can go to places that no human can safely go, like the surface of Venus — or the outer Solar system and beyond; can help us learn things about space we could not learn from Earth	Individual probes can be expensive and take a long time to develop; launch rockets can leave debris that can fall to Earth; probes take long time to travel to places where they can send us information we want

More Books About Space Garbage

Here are more books that contain information about objects in our Solar system. If you are interested in them, look for them in your library or bookshop.

The Asteroids by Isaac Asimov (Gareth Stevens, 1989)
Comets and Meteors by Isaac Asimov (Gareth Stevens, 1989)
Our Solar System by Isaac Asimov (Gareth Stevens, 1989)
Rockets, Probes, and Satellites by Isaac Asimov (Gareth Stevens, 1989)
Space Laboratories by Gregory L. Vogt (Franklin Watts, 1988)
Space Satellites by Gregory L. Vogt (Franklin Watts, 1987)
Spaceships by Gregory L. Vogt (Franklin Watts, 1988)
Space Walking by Gregory L. Vogt (Franklin Watts, 1986)

Places to Visit

You can explore outer space — including the places close to our planet where space litter is becoming more and more of a problem — without leaving Earth.

Jodrell Bank Visitors' Centre
Macclesfield, Cheshire

Science Museum
S. Kensington, London

London Planetarium
Marylebone Road,
London

London Schools Planetarium
Wandsworth School
Sutherland Grove, London

Royal Observatory
Edinburgh, Scotland

There are also planetaria at museums in Southend, Liverpool, National Maritime Museum, Greenwich (London), Armagh Observatory (N. Ireland), and Mills Observatory, Dundee (Scotland).

For More Information About Space Garbage

Here are some places you can write to for more information about the things we put up in space. Be sure to tell them exactly what you want to know about. Remember to include your age, full name, and address.

For information about planetary missions:
NASA Jet Propulsion Laboratory
Public Affairs 180-201
4800 Oak Grove Drive
Pasadena, California 91109, USA

About Strategic Defense Initiative (SDI, Star Wars):
Assistant Secretary of Defense for Public Affairs
Public Correspondence Branch, Room 2E777
Pentagon
Washington, DC 20301, USA